thirst of pisces

thirst of pisces

poems

kate march

atmosphere press

contents

i. The Dawning (Surrender)

ii. The Flow (Movements)

iii. The Stillness (Disruptions)

the dawning

(Surrender)

AND...
Dominican Republic

She dwells in the arms of opportunity
Cradled by songs of freedom.
Her hair undone as the tension
Living in her wrists
And, long fingers.

Her long fingers grip at glittering light
Cascading through the morning clouds,
They move as if gently communing
With a baby grand piano.
She peers up at those who watch over.
Smiling, she falls at their winged feet,
Genuflecting to silent symphonies, a newfound resolve.

She transformed everything,
Vacuuming up
Dust, mire, and cobwebs.
She bore a shield and wore
A soft, but hardy armor so she could
Conquer all that would
Tumble towards her body, her heart,
And, her space.

Opened by the winds of change,
Her dance evokes the infinite.
He wants a part of it,
She was quite unsure of that.

IN PLACE OF BLOOD (THERE WAS ICE)
Iceland

In place of blood,
baby blue ice.

In place of freckled flesh,
the blackest of sand.

In place of a warm embrace,
the north wind.

In place of mouths and eyes,
peaks and caves.

In place of me,
vast, wild horizon.

In place of you,
distant emerald seas.

In place of us,
the universe.

In place of nothing,
everything.

In place of ending,
everlasting.

SORAYA
London, England

After a grueling week
I step
Into the tub.
Sometimes,
She reads to me,
As I soak and stew
For hours.

I pull the plug
And sit there.
Immersed in my old skin,
I watch the lukewarm water
Spiral down the drain —
It is a ritual.

She wraps me up
In her scrappy blue towel
And warms me with her
Storytelling.
Her spindly finger
Caresses my cheek
As she whispers,
"Your skin is as soft as rose petals."

Before bath time
My muscles and bones
Ache in fear and filth.
I feel dirty
As dreams and disappointments
Imploded within.
She washes me pure.

REBIRTH
London, England

Before —
I try to move my hands and arms, but I am paralyzed. I want to shout, but I produce no sound. I sense people near or around me, but I can't see their bodies. From up above, I see myself down there: unmoving and knocked out. (I recall not liking that stillness; it wasn't a familiar me.) As I peer closer, I see the me below is simply remnants of time, a discarded exoskeleton. Maybe I molted that outer shell in order to escape, re-locate, and start again.

During —
It's a ride, like time travel through some other realm. The journey has some ups and some downs all the while rushing towards a brightness. I am restless yet curious. By the near end, I am reaching out; my invisible limbs pulling me towards some simmering hope. I am extending to a voice that calls me back, but I'm not sure where back is. Then, I realize, one voice became two voices pulling me in different directions. There is something I want to go to and something I don't want to leave. I feel torn between 2 places, 2 shells, and 2 selves. This must be limbo. Suddenly, I hear a third voice, my own voice, loud and consuming: I must go back! Take me back, please! Take me to myself, the self that has more room to grow.

After —
I return. I slowly regain my force, the power that pulses through us all. It flows from my toenails all the way up to my hair's split ends. My steps slowly become sure again. I cough. I cry. I laugh. I dance. I promise to be more diligent. Not that I felt alone in limbo. I wasn't. I sensed others caught there as well. We were all caught in a sticky situation of choice: to grow here and now or there and then; in micro-steps or within the infinite macro. But now, I begin to understand. I am the pilot steering the voyage no matter where, who, or what I go to or leave. I am the human hermit crab, growing the shell until I feel constricted by my own growth. The physical shell is only a temporary home, but it is my home to protect in the meantime.

Now —
My sweaty flesh wakes me up. Yawning, I hear an echo as I'm still shaking off the bizarre, groggy fugue state I was trapped within. It says, "Choose the path that honors your soul — life after life after life after life, shell after shell after shell after shell." I open my eyes and I'm awake now, fully. One day I'll be ready for a new skin, a thicker casing, my next rebirth. For now, I am here, learning, growing, dreaming, defending.

NO BODY
Cairo, Egypt

Faceless women
Roam without
A visible body.
No body means
Nobody.

the flow

(Movements)

THE BENCH BY THE WATER
Kennedy Town, Hong Kong

The air is fresh.
The air is heavy.
The air anticipates you.

My tears are fresh.
My tears are heavy.
My tears anticipate you.

AFTER THE STORM
Sai Ying Pun, Hong Kong

Thunder claps, the sky divides,
The rain pours
Down, down.
The wind frantically whips
My hair from port to starboard.
I am standing still, waiting for
Your hand to join mine.
I whisper to the heavens
And urge fate to take control.
I start to dance in the MUD,
I am cold and shivering, but
The mere thought of you
Keeps me warm, keeps me warm.

The stars stopped moving,
Hanging there,
Also, waiting.
They were shining brightly
For you, for you.
Deep into midnight and beyond,
Our dreams slipped into the grasp
Of reality and we stood there,
Watching each other from afar,
Our lips found each other
Even in darkness, even in darkness.

Tears fall down to the soggy Earth,
Waterfalls of joy and sadness, both.
The salt dried my cheeks and
Made me recall the time we
Sat in the desert dunes,
Conjuring up the magic of our future,
Our love deepening by the hour,
Our souls flying far, far far
Away and up into the sunrise.
Together forever, together forever.

FREE
Victoria Peak, Hong Kong

I see
The edge,
In the horizon.
I sprint
Full force,
Ready to fly,
Ready to rise.
Pegasus and Phoenix,
As one.
Born from fire,
Alive in the wind...
I am free.

GREYNESS
Victoria Peak & Sai Ying Pun, Hong Kong

I have this particular bench with this particular view — it's my favorite. I've seen that view in the morning, sunset, summer, winter, torrential rains... I've seen it in crystal clear, blue skies. And you know, it never interests me more than when it's a grey day.

A few months back, I'm at my favorite spot and it's a quintessential grey day: I mean the perfect blend of sunlight and cloudiness. I take in my familiar surroundings and suddenly in greyness, everything seems vibrant, real, — palpable. I notice the distant boats, the ones I always saw, anchored there in the water— floating in stillness...somehow in greyness, even from so far away, I discern their micro shifts...In each small sway, I feel them preparing for their next journey. My senses were turned on. My perception of the horizon shifted and changed. That experience became a strong metaphor. It reminds me to embrace greyness. Because when we locate ourselves in the grey, we can discover true momentum.

Now, grey is not typically a popular color. Grey refers to those murky "in-between spaces" in life that are tricky to navigate. Greyness is unpredictability, ambiguity, uncertainty. It's perplexing...kind of intimidating. The thing is though grey areas simply require a different kind of navigation system. Rather than black and white logic of linear routes, pre-programmed paths, or fixed destinations, greyness calls for deeper exploration and curiosity. Traveling in grey necessitates instinct, emotions, intuition, and all of the senses.

My own journey with greyness began as a student. I was studying both dance and neuroscience, but was fiercely set on becoming a doctor. I did the pre-med routine: early morning chemistry labs, hospital internships, summer research... Then, when I was 20, I took my first flight ever and went to live and study in Copenhagen. I immersed myself in the novelties of new cultures and tasted the sweetness of independence. By chance, my host family owned a dance studio — and I witnessed firsthand, a tenacious, lifelong devotion to the arts. When I look back to that first trip to Europe, I can't recall one instant in particular where I made the decision to embrace greyness. The experience as a whole was like one big epiphany, a moment of rebirth. I returned home — inspired. I said goodbye to medicine. I allowed my passion for dance to lead me in a more fuzzy direction. My grey voyage continued and eventually led me to London... I completed a Master's degree in choreography. Then, I spent time traveling, exploring, having adventures in almost 40 countries, living on 3 continents, and all the while honing my interests in dance, immersive theatre, site-specific performance, and the overall artistic process. I've realized: flowing with greyness elicits a different world view. Crystallized definitions of success and failure dissolve. You are no longer motivated by perfectionism. You are not confined by any boxes or strict trajectories. You are limitless. Accepting greyness means being willing to take risks, disrupt conventions, and carve your own path.

Over time, I ended up in Hong Kong, my interests all collided...

Can you think of an experience that deeply moved you? Falling in love; a beautiful painting; an inspiring conversation; a film...Something that unlocked your imagination, opened your heart, made you feel human. For me, it is the act of live performance. Performing and connecting to a live audience gives me a feeling beyond words: it's magic. I want people to feel this magic. It's what drives me, it's what drives my vision for my work. As I've come to learn, magic doesn't happen with prescribed methods. You can't plan for it or control it. In fact, profound moments can ONLY be realized through embracing greyness. If you want to feel experience something indescribable, then you have to follow instincts rather than formulas. I do this in my creative practice. I use improvisation and spontaneity to breath freedom and playfulness into each piece painting, each poem, each production. Sometimes I abandon scripts or change choreography to adapt to the context or the mood of a particular audience. In this way, the exchanges between audience and performer (or writer) are powerful, personal, unconventional, and authentic...indescribable.

Embracing greyness is the difference between ordinary and captivating between flying and soaring. Flowing with greyness, you allow for that spark of magic. This is true in performance and art, but also in contexts like business, innovation, relationships...life in general. Accepting greyness means engaging in what feels meaningful to you and through this discovering new frontiers. Look, I'm no stranger to self-doubt. I have faced the uncomfortable challenges of personal and professional growth, of grey areas...Many times and many times to come I retreat back into the arms of a black and white perspective hoping to be cradled by certainty. But, welcoming greyness or warmly greeting the enigmas and complexities of life, immediately flexes innate muscles of strength, courage, and trust — muscles that exist in everyone. So exercise those muscles, recognize and push through your fears, trust the present moment, and embrace the unknown. When you do this, at least for me, I find something stronger and more gratifying than safety and comfort — I find my voice. I find my convictions. I find myself. Accepting greyness means striving for presence not perfection and appreciating the messiness and the beauty of self-transformation.

It is time to acknowledge the immense value that exists in promoting a horizon not only of blue skies and crystal clear answers, but also one of open-ended possibilities and that special, mysterious, murkiness of greyness. Grey has infinite shades — it's elusive. Sure, it's a little intimidating, but more than that, it's intriguing...Grey is exquisite because it's undefinable. Honor your instincts. Respect your intuition and emotions. Be enthusiastically present. Be undefinable. Embrace greyness and embrace the most beautifully messy and most worthwhile journey you will ever know...the journey of becoming you.

PULSES
Bali, Indonesia

My chest —
Beat
So loud.
I mistook
The pulsations
As invitations
To dance.
When really,
The rhythms
Conducted a farewell
Processional.

ALONE IN CAMPS BAY
Cape Town, South Africa

The sky burns with red, orange, and pink.
The wine is smoky.
The stars are blooming.
The water kisses the colors.
I forgive myself.
Once and for all.

SUNSET IV
Stellenbosch, South Africa

At the end of the Earth.
The sun was falling.
The blanket of stars
Expanding infinitely,
Rapidly.

You were not with me.
I was there sipping
Sanguine wine all alone.
I drank up freedom.
I consumed melancholy.
I washed down curiosity, too.

In that particular sunset,
I wondered— who would
One day understand
The depths of such
Kairos?

A perfect moment of solitude.
A perfect moment of limitless possibility.
A moment I look back on with pure
Gratitude.

SPRING BLOSSOMS
Ho Chi Minh City, Vietnam

Spring blossoms- fragrant,
Reminiscent
Of the love
We used to share.

Spring blossoms- ripe,
Pretty for plucking.
Or, like us,
Ready to fall.

IN PEKING
Beijing, China

red lipstick
red nail polish
red cheeks
red shoes
red roses
red red red.

red chopsticks
red book
red pipe
red lantern
red sunset
red red red.

red scarf
red bag
red meat
red hat
red heart
red red red.

red chairs
red light
red bicycle
red envelope
red throat
red red red.

red ink
red stamp
red hands
red flag
red blood
red red r—

HUTONGS
Beijing, China

We walk into the mouth
Of the maze.
Darkness creeps near.
We walk forward into the arms
Of the labyrinth.

The twists,
Unavoidable.
The turns,
Nauseating.
I smile.
You laugh.

We turn right,
We twist left,
Led by invisible red threads,
We walk fearlessly,
Into the unknown ether.

Together —
We were never lost.
Apart —
We are nowhere to be found.

SOUR STOMACH; SWEET MEMORY
Angkor Wat, Cambodia

You are
The other side
Of infinity.
I know
The color of your eyes
Better than anyone
You will ever meet.
You are the head
To my tail.
I know
The flavor of your soul.
It's a taste acquired
By few.
By me.
We leave each other
Undone.
And, understood.

IN KHAO LAK (REBUILDING)
Khao Lak, Thailand

I look back
In the moist sand.
My lonesome footsteps
Replaced
By forgiving tides —
Seeking refuge
In their own
Demise.

CHRONOS & KAIROS
Bangkok, Thailand & Hong Kong

A few weeks ago, I was in paradise, on a remote beach. I was sitting on a swing right on the water's edge. It was stunning. The power of the waves crashing. The expansiveness of the horizon. The clouds shifting shapes. And God, that glorious golden light of pinks, oranges, and purples.

I am not uncomfortable with flying solo — In fact, I cherished the solitude and the deep serenity in that alone moment... But I find myself replaying that hour in my mind ... and my heart retaliates, reminding me how special a shared sunset is too. I've been lucky to have experienced cosmic collisions of inexplicable emotions. I've felt the transforming heat from the electric flame of affairs and relationships... But, I want to feel the burn of a flame that can't be extinguished. I want the trick birthday candle kind of love. No matter how hard you try, the fire keeps rekindling itself. You see, I am on this continued, perpetuating and perplexing quest for a love that sustains me across time and across space.

Perhaps this is why I've started to conceive of love into different forms in the same way that the Ancient Greeks separated time into 2 forms: chronos & kairos.

Now, chronos refers to duration, length of time, a sequence of moments that elapse. Chronos —is measured in seconds, minutes, and hours, days and months and years. I think of chronos love when I see my friends who are engaged or married. My parents who have been together for 35 years. Or my grandparents who have been together for 60. Chronos love tends to be the more widely coveted and valued love in society Probably because it gives preference to linear time and physical togetherness and the stability of knowing we aren't alone.

The beauty of chronos love stems from its projection into the realm we understand - along a horizontal axis that parallels our own existence. The journey, though immensely fickle and fallible, reflects our own journey of becoming -perhaps, chronos love, with all its conventions and formalities and inherent commitments - perhaps, braving such helps us endure ourselves with all our own flaws, chaos, and imperfections.

Chronos love has largely been a fugitive love for me. I have felt the tugging desire for it, but I've only ever really been on the outskirts of chronos. I guess the reason I have wrestled with it is that it can seem all too finite and confining. It feels like I surrender to time... or our relative lack of it.. It's scary to yield to our own humanity.

Chronos love is the ultimate commitment of time and space, but let's not forget commitment doesn't necessitate love. Only love necessitates love. Let's not fall into the trap of thinking that longing for commitment precedes love. Love is and always will be — the only precedent.

Which is why kairos is so important.

Kairos, implies a different type of time – a less literal, but really significant time, in my opinion. It's qualitative; it's the metaphysical. Kairos is that magical instant in which time stands still. It's the supreme moment. Sparks flying. What does Kairos translate into in the context of love? This is a destination I've frequented. Impulse and spontaneity. When frequencies seem to match instantaneously. That perfect evening of perfect dialogue, perfect challenges, perfect sex, and perfect energy. A perfect moment where one can't help but feel -- breathless. Maybe that's enough for me up until now. Maybe all I've really ever pursued and received is just a series of intense and intoxicating tornadoes of connection. I am grateful for the experience however brief they were by the clock's definition. Because fleeting instances of no obligation, no expectation, and no responsibility... Well, that makes life feel eternal. Even when and especially when we know the reality is otherwise.

The hassle with being human and experiencing kairos is that it disappears. It's then, at that vanishing point where the cardinal message lurking in the shadows starts to rear... kidnapping jubilation and pulling us down to flesh and earth again: *it wasn't meant to be.*

Kairos is hot....and exquisite... until you want more. And most of us, we want more. The conundrum of love is of course in reality we want magic and in magic, we want reality. Time and love, they are not as proportional or rational or linear as we tend to convince ourselves. What about the verticality of the love - how deep is the love? How far down does it reach or how far into the heavens does it fly? If we can tease out the relationship between love, time, space, and connection, we can decide for ourselves HOW we love; WHY we love; and WHEN we love. When we value love beyond our own human limitations of time and physical presence, maybe then and only then does commitment become our right. And maybe, also then, the short term affairs and the long term relationships become equally meaningful and beautiful. Maybe, then, our happiness doesn't feel reliant on commitment or not being alone, but feels reinforced by it like an additional piece of our own individual puzzle. Seeking or finding love, be it chronos or kairos, depends on who we are, and where we are along our own time-space continuum and whose continuum intersects with our own...

Where are you on your own journey? What kind of love are you seeking? What do you desire? The invincibility and timelessness of kairos or the substance and endurance of chronos? Is it possible to find a love that surpasses these distinctions or blends them?

I hope so.

All I can say is:
Be curious about the immeasurability of love. Be curious about the ability of love to transcend the restrictions of earthly existence. Be curious as to how love can fit into the conditions of such as well. Be profoundly grateful with any love- whether it's an instant or a lifetime. Yearn for unconditional love. Yearn for the disruption and the magic of it, the pain and the pleasure, the adventures and the conventions. For God's sake, yearn for shared sunsets.

Whether it's chronos or kairos or something in between, love grants us the illusion of forever. And despite knowing forever is impossible, I'll keep searching for the right person to share a sunset with... a person who makes me feel that perhaps I've discovered the other side of infinity.

OPENING NIGHT
Kennedy Town, Hong Kong

after all
the emotions. all
the writing. all
the stories. all
the messages. all
the bullshit. all
the anxiety. all
the insomnia. all
the struggles with self-worth. all
the battlefields. all
the fucking. all
the heartache. all
the loneliness. all
the victories. after all
the rainbows. all
the storms. all
the long walks. all
the flights. all.
the turbulence. all
the laughter. all
the wine. all
the tears. after all
the poetry. all
the benches. all
the sunsets. all
the dancing. all
of me, all of me. after all
of my voice. all
of my full heart. all
of my empty heart. all
of my blood. all
of my sweat. all
of my sunshine. after all
of it,
I am.

FALLING...
Sydney, Australia

In Love.
Down.
Over.
Backwards.
Asleep.
For you.

BALCONY
Phuket, Thailand

I sit on my balcony
With a hot cup of
Jasmine cha.
Watching the world
As it rises from slumber.
The peace and serenity
This grants me
Is unfathomable —
A gift from the angels.
Then, taking a moment
From my mesmerizing
Outward meditation,
I scan around
And see more balconies
With other people
Sitting down
Breathing in the
Morning dew
Drinking cups of
All kinds of tea.
Together we are
Worshipping
In the most beautiful
Of cathedrals.

SHINY BLACK COFFIN
Bangkok, Thailand

I dreamt
I closed
The lid
Of my own
Shiny black coffin.
A former self
Had passed away.

I dragged
The burden
Through the streets
Of my childhood
Seeking
A burial ground.
The dead weight
Of the past
Is a heavy load.
But I'm ready
To lay it
To rest.

Give me
The plot of Earth
Next to
My former heartache,
Alongside
The deceased fears
That used to choke
My well-being
And my pursuit
Of love.
The time has come
To lower the skeleton
Of what used to be
Into the eternal
Wormhole of lost youth.

As mother and daughter
Accept the beauty
Of new blossoms
With a ripened fragrance
Signaling
The evolution of self,
The breath of air
Which sustains
This goodbye
Is sweeter than most,
Longer than most.
And when the pink
light from the setting
Sun of this season
Draws closer
To the horizon,
May we all return
To the bounty
Of this resting place
With comforting
Slivers of remembrance
Sticking themselves
Within our minds
Within our souls
If only for an instant
Before we pull them out.

The hovering thunderclouds
Threaten our peace.
But as we all
Come to discover,
The rain delivers
Salvation
Just as
The tears grant us
Solidarity
In our own
Relentlessly sorrowful
Relentlessly joyful
Circles of rebirth.

OUR BLUE BLOOD
New Orleans, Louisiana

These blues
Just won't be destroyed.
These deep, Stygian hues
Cannot be ignored.
Because — they were
Born in my roots.

My heart pumps,
So thirstily.
My body aches,
For serenity.
My teeth clench,
In hopes of repose.

I can feel my skin
Searching for comfort
And a peace
I am unsure exists.
But, it's not all darkness.
More like — incessant sensitivity.

My yin yang vulnerability:
Bottomless strength of the ocean's tides
And, the fragility of a glass
Perched on a windy rooftop;
Threatening to break
Into a million and one pieces.

My mother.
My mother's mother.
My father's mother and hers.
And so on and so forth and so was.
Always fighting courageously,
All on the same kind of battlefield.

The internal crusades took a toll.
Wounds run deep.
Scars are ageless and timeless, it seems.
I am still fighting.
With them and
For them.

At times, I feel like a prisoner
Of my blood's bloodless war.
Most times, I award myself
A medal of bravery.
These blues are blossoming
Into a rich journey of color.

UNDER|WATER
Lake Muskoka, Canada

Nothing feels certain
But the cool wind
On my face
And the sea salt
Dancing in my hair.

I'm always feeling strange
When the moon is full.
But tonight,
I am
Out of sorts —
Sort of like
I was cut in half
With my heart floating
Beyond this galaxy
In a clouded, shrouded
Lonely place.

Other parts of me
Are running—
No destination in mind
Wanting to disappear.
Dizzying myself
From a piercing desire to disguise
The pain of wanting for
Everything and nothing
All at once.

I am swallowed whole
By my own mouth.
Drowning in
A river of emotions,
The peace
Of my dreams
Flooding.

Over and over, I beg
The strawberry moon
Have mercy on me,
On them.

Why moon must you
Pull me like the water?
Back and forth
To and fro I go
Waltzing incessantly
Without resting my weary feet.
I'm tired and ill at ease.
I want to both sleep for days
And move for months.
I never know which
Suits me better.

I am divided and looking for
That which will reunite
My yin and my yang.
I torque my torso
To get a better look
A closer look at my
Feisty reflection.
Decidedly, there is no
Better life than mine.
And, still the teardrops fall
From time to time to time.
I think the water needs
My replenishment and I honor
Its every request— because:
It is forever my redeemer.

I open my eyes to the sky
And let the blues consume me.
My arms open wide,
I whisper to my dearest friend:
I'll spit myself out

Piece by piece
But only if you promise
Please put me back together.
Take me under.
Under the surface.
Underneath my fears.
Under your wings.
Take me all the way under,
Give me refuge
In the fluidity of your mysteries.

Under I go.
Over and under.
Slowly and then all at once.

SHE HELPED ME MOVE ON
Victoria Peak, Hong Kong

I remember now.
I trek up and up and up.
Ten thousand hikes up and down
To the city's natural spire.
In the beginning,
Angels carried me.
Heavy heart and all.

I remember now.
The ritual footfalls like
Personal pilgrimages.
The more steps,
The more sweat,
The more strength—
The more I return
To myself.

I remember now.
Each footprint, cathartic.
Each bench stop, reflective.
Each sky, therapeutic.
I honor that mountain
For her nurturing presence.
She helped me move on.

A NEW PRAYER
Air Transit Over the North Pole

He makes

Me love

My flaws

Amen.

THE KNIGHT
Mui Wo, Lantau Island, Hong Kong

He made me accustomed to a love that felt uneasy. He made me feel a love that was complex and unfinished and unyielding. He tricked me into believing it was true. He gave me a love that was conditional and wrapped it up as unconditional. I believed him. He duped me into thinking he was my soulmate, my one true love. He kidnapped my love and held it hostage. His demand was that I change my perspective and give him time — *my* time.

He led me to believe that love could be all joy, a cool relief from the blazing difficulties of this world, an oasis to drink from, a place to hide not to be lost, but only to be found, was false. He said: *forget it all.* My captor made me think the best kind of love was always tragic and unrealized. With every breath, word, laugh, smile, chat, he convinced me deeper and deeper that real love hurt. He coaxed me to endure the pain, he forced me into a dungeon of false truths. I spiraled and fell into a darkness like no other. I came undone.

Then, I met him.

A hero. No shiny sword. No white horse. He's not a prince. I'm no damsel in distress either. But, he rescued me. He helped me escape the tyranny of my chains. Chains which were reinforced by accumulated distortions that had become my laws. The chains kept me from real freedom, real love, real self-worth. They shackled me to grief and unanswered questions. This new man broke those chains.

And, when the chains left open sores on my wrists and on my sternum, he licked them clean. He gave me water to drink and encouraged me to walk out of the dark pit that I had been thrown into and grown attached to for so long. That pit had become my safety and comfort; at one time, it was everything. But in truth, it was a place where dreams met their death.

My new champion guided me to the light and I felt revived. For a time, he became my oxygen until I could breathe on my own. He helped me heal myself- a true knight. His armor wasn't flawlessly shiny, but it was strong. The armor is good and decent he told me, but it's not impenetrable. Nothing is. He showed me that no shield is mighty enough to fend ourselves from life's sharpness and unavoidable trickeries. The only way to become the strongest warrior is to understand what the edge of a sword feels like when it pierces the flesh. And even more importantly, each warrior must know how the wound heals — the only way that wounds ever scar — through the one and only treatment that underlines all recovery and all destruction too — time.

Give this time, he said, and you will see the lessons of your wounds through the beauty of your scars. And with that, he kissed my scars. He said he couldn't imagine me without them — they made me who I am: a fierce woman with stories to share.

And in that moment, when the sun was just starting to kiss the ocean, I realized the depth of knowledge imparted by my former imprisonment. In that instance and in many instances to come, through the grace of time, I would come to know real love - an unconditional love - a love with more wholeness and liberty than I ever knew was possible. I discovered clarity through a love full of light. I drank from its cup of purity each day. I found a love that was restorative and regenerative. This was the fountain of youth. This was what my heart was always seeking as the one and only truth — love has no boundaries.

Love will never greedily take time from you, it will always give you time. Before this you will think that time is limited, but when real love flows through your blood, you will know, in love, there are no conditions - time is limitless, you are limitless. A true warrior, like a true knight, will only ever fight through and with love.

When I dropped down to my knees at the water's edge, as the last light of day made it possible to see my scars, I felt the water touching my skin and I felt the corpse of the past float away from me. I looked up at my knight, with tears of joy, and I was speechless. My mouth opened, but I could find no words. His gentle yet powerful force brought me back from the brink of death, from the flames of heartache and unbearable suffering.

His arms became a blanket of protection that kept me warm and happy. I told him he was everything to me. I told him I wanted to give him everything, but I had nothing left to give. I had believed at one point this kind of love was a love for which I was undeserving and unworthy.

He dropped down next to me so that we were both at the mercy of the ocean's tides. He kissed me and I saw his scars too. He whispered in my ear: *You give everything when you give love.*

We stood up and held each other in the peaceful darkness hearing only the push and pull of the moon through the crashing waves. We just stood there. In stillness. Together. For a long time. With love, with freedom. And it was there, time also stood still.

Love does conquer all.

the stillness

(Disruptions)

HUMANE RAYS OF A PAINLESS DAWN
Brooklyn, New York

Darkness grew
Inside of me.
A black web
Of scathing scars
Attaching quite aptly
To my livelihood,
To my womanhood,
Dangerously, destructively —
A venomous creature
Pulling my body
Down, way down.
Into an abyss
I feared had
No exit sign.

Darkness thrived
Inside of me.
Without logic,
This gruesome thing
Wove a warpath.
Leaving not a trace
Of light or peace.
Further we fell,
My body and my spirit.
Fearful and entangled
In a bloody mess —
Enduring
An open-ended chapter
Of grueling soreness.

Darkness survived
Inside of me.
I can't recall
A time
When it didn't
Take my breath away.

Toss my hope away.
Push me over the edge.
It spoon-fed me
Shame and distress.
Hoping I would be
Too full up to disturb
The comfort
Of our anti-symbiosis duress.

Then, darkness died.
Finally.
One sunny spring day.
It wasn't an easy
Downfall.
In its absence
I woke up slowly —
Groggy and perplexed.
A temporary fog,
The welcome successor
Replacing sadness, bitterness
And angry, clenched fists.

When the murk subsided,
A crystal clarity and poignant power
Birthed
A deep wisdom for survival.
I felt unburdened and lighter.
We rose — body and soul,
From that abominable abyss.
Like twin Phoenix birds,
Free and floating,
Back into the humane rays
Of a painless dawn.

PAST LIFE PAIN
New York, New York

One century and a half or so ago
My soul's shell died
During childbirth.
I must have tried
To hold on;
To hold the infant.
But my womb
Shattered and bled out.
Murdering my possibility
Of motherhood.
My spirit grieves—still.
The grief poisons
Still.

In another era,
I was royal.
My only purpose —
Bring forth heirs.
I failed 10 times.
My insides were
Rotten.
I prayed for forgiveness.
Dark ugly circles emerged,
Blackness,
Under and inside my eyes.
Fatigued from sadness.
In the recesses
Of my now subconscious
I remember the tears.
In fact, I can't forget.
My body won't allow it.
Not yet.

The other former life
Revealed to me,
Through suffering,
Happened in ancient Italy.
I lived under the shadow

Of a sleepy volcano.
As it slowly awoke
From a long slumber,
I ran like the wind.
Hysterical with anxiety.
I gathered my babies
In my arms.
Afraid to lose them;
Panic consumed me.
But the other villagers
Sauntered calmly.
No need for alarm.
Ultimately, after days of worry,
I didn't lose my children
But, I did lose my peace.
I guess I am still trying to find it.

Past lives
Haunt my body.
Deep, deep down
My pelvis swells.
Turmoil manifests
Into sharp moments
Of toxic torment.
Teeth clenched,
I bear the fear
And deep-rooted shame.
I listen to it,
But I no longer feed it.
This life will be recalled
Differently.

I hope.

ON DEATH
New York, New York

The universe is
An infinitely tiered
Red velvet cake.
Devour it,
Indulge in it.
Not just a little slice
Or even a generous helping.
No, child,
Put down the fork.
Use both hands and dig into
The delicious, gifted crumbs
Of pulse and breath.

With a glass of whole milk,
Half full.
Open your eyes and tastebuds,
Appreciate the many flavors of truth
That this plate holds for you.
As the tick-tock
Looming of
That great finale—
The for-ever,
Infinite absence —
A gloriously messy
Full expression
Of the unknown,
Echoes in the kitchen.

You have permission to be ravenous,
Embrace an appetite.
Lick the frosting from the golden spoon.
And although,
The inevitably vacant silver platter
Seems like a frightening, fasting darkness
In fact, there will be more, sweetness, sugar.
Within the vacuum
Of nothingness —
We are everything.

The cosmos
Becomes us.
And we become
Pure light—
Timeless
And, unshackled.
Let them eat cake.
Let yourself eat cake.

Now and not tomorrow,
As I sit and dream
Under the summer's setting sun,
I strive to thrive by
Naturally savoring
In tremendously temporary
Existences and puddings
Delighting in the mysterious taste
Of authentic beauty,
Courageous joy,
And, real love.

SEED. BLOOM. DECAY.
Sedona, Arizona

I witness the bittersweetness
Of the cherry blossoms'
Descent
From limb to ground
And I believe
I am the cherry blossom
In seed,
In bloom,
In decay.
I believe too —
We are autumn's leaves;
We are winter's snow —
Enduring states of change,
Flowering fully,
Accepting transformation,
Falling gracefully
From high heights.

HIDDEN
Brooklyn, New York

Some mornings,
I paint the town
In deep, divine reds.
Nothing stands in my way.
Everything touches my spirit,
In an ecstatic lushness.
Like a spoonful of honey
Slowly slipping onto my tongue.
I carry so much
Passion
In the palm of my hand.
It might explode
Into the hearts
Of everyone I encounter.

This body is a battlefield.
This love is a revolution.
Eyes are not the only windows...

Some mornings,
I am slammed shut.
Soaked in the hues
Of an inky indigo; a bottomless twilight.
Swallowed by something
I can't quite name.
An untitled tether
Attaching my guts to a gnawing
Esoteric ache.
As my hair greys,
I sip the darkness,
Like a hot mint tea,
Carefully, quietly —
To endure is to transform.

This body is a battlefield.
This love is a revolution.
Eyes are not the only entrance...

Other mornings,
The dream state
Washes the waking hours
In exuberance.
I shout in violets;
Laugh in yellows;
Banter in chartreuse.
Like a bird,
Gliding on the sea breeze;
I am carefree and I ride
The peaks and troughs
With ease and peace.
I'm still hidden,
But what you can't see,
You feel.

This body is a battlefield.
This love is a revolution.
Eyes are not the only way in...

CHARLESTON MORNINGS
Charleston, South Carolina

The majestic oak tree
Watches over us.
We are safe
Under the net
Of her many arms.
With her supple strength
And fierce resilience,
She bends —
Never breaks.
I look out at her
And wonder
What has she seen?
What has she felt?

The seasons
Change her
From the inside out.
She signals
The metamorphosis
With beauty abound.
We celebrate
Time & timelessness
Through her.
For her.
Her leaves may fall,
Yet she stands tall.
What have we seen?
What have we felt?

THE TAXI DRIVER
Tokyo, Japan

I arrive
At the train station
In the blitz of
A rampant rush hour.
Three heavy bags,
Jet-lag jello legs,
No cell service,
Post-honeymoon glow,
Desperate to be horizontal.
Welcome to Tokyo.

I follow
Arrows and instinct
Searching for the way out
Without any sign(s)
Of my native tongue.
A dizzying odyssey of
Long corridors and stairways
Winding me up, over,
Around and down
Yielding to construction sites
And homeward bound bodies.
Welcome to Tokyo.

I yearn
For saké, sushi, and slumber,
As I feel the city's
Lights come into focus.
The air hits me and I gulp
Some personal space.
Thankfully
Some nice man senses my
Disorientation and guided me
Like my north star
Towards the taxi queue.
He brokenly whispers,
Welcome to Tokyo.

I exhale
Making it to the car with
The gentle, kind elder
With warm eyes,
Driving with gloves.
He turns to face me
Smiling, he speaks
(In Japanese)
And after a pregnant pause,
And mutual confusion,
We belly laugh together.

I share the screenshot
Of the hotel name.
Fifteen minutes passed
We just sat there
Attempting clairvoyance.
When finally after more grins
And some giddy giggling,
He somehow deciphers
My destination.
It is a holy moment.
Hallelujah.
Welcome to Tokyo.

DRINK THE DESERT'S WINTER
Santa Fe, New Mexico

The Desert
Surprises me.
I tend to feel
Unbridled
In its abundant
Otherworldly
Emptiness.
My throat tightens
Thirsty for freedom.
Waiting to encounter
Georgia's ghost.
Rain down on my
Small world.
Space is our
Greatest milk and honey.

One crisp
February morning,
My lungs sting
As I make my way
Up to the sky-high hill.
The fresh snow
Crushes beneath my feet.
I gather some
In my naked, cold hand
And watch
The molecules melt leisurely.
My tongue
Yearns for that liquid beauty.
Could this moment
Be my fountain of youth?
If I sip
This landscape
And spit it out in words,
Will you hear my voice forever?

29 EPIPHANIES FROM FOUND WORDS
New York & Portugal

I. Find real guidance from feeling good.
II. Shift anxiety into empowered inspiration.
III. Celebrate kindness in everything.
IV. Go deep with purpose — a turning point.
V. Repair cosmic harmony (for her).
VI. Praise grit and goodness.
VII. Look to the higher self for peace and peace of mind. Make the body your guide.
VIII. Time alone in the clouds is time well spent.
IX. In the long run un-compromised joy is fierce.
X. The great sleep awaits — find your dreams now.
XI. Leading your lost wild heart home will transform your art.
XII. Simple inspiration: light, mountain, sun, moon, sea, trees, the earth.
XIII. Sisterhood. Women helping women.
XIV. Embrace the future big breakthroughs of women.
XV. The essence of human grace and power — menstrual period blood.
XVI. The truth is: angels always illuminate the darkness.
XVII. Fight an infamously painful condition through breath.
XVIII. Seasons of progress matter.
XIX. Perfection is miserable.
XX. Honor the inner impulse.
XXI. Face yourself with defiant love.
XXII. Dance to understand and feel the beautiful magic of the stars.
XXIII. Consider curing the world and women with gratitude vibes.
XXIV. The real secret power is heat energy on the body.
XXV. Channel decades of unbearable pain into art. (Feel brave.)
XXVI. Maybe just appreciate this venomous moderate to severe hysterical female all-natural human pain. (Every woman is a queen.)
XXVII. The pursuit of comfort, comfort, comfort, comfort, comfort, comfort.

XXVIII. Mindfully trust the hidden power of relief in the body
— ENDORPHINS.

IN THE CHAIR IN THE PHOENIX MALL
Chennai, India

My mouth is bone dry
From the Indian heat,
The jet lag fatigue,
The existential exhaustion.
Most people require
Ten glasses of clean water
To live in this climate.
That means, for me,
No amount of drinking
Will prevent my body's
Dehydration.

I feel bitter about
My corporeal sensitivities.
And, alongside my envy
Of people who aren't
As fragile as me —
I am plagued by
A relentless internal chatter.
Indeed, my mind races.
Constantly, these days.
Savage.

I ask myself:
Am I doing enough?
Am I being enough?
Am I good enough?
I tell my inner voice:
Enough!
But I don't listen very well.
Trips this far from home
Inevitably carry the weight
Of heavy self-reflections.

Feelings of gratitude
Surface regularly
And also, feelings of,

Is this the life
I always imagined?
Paths have
So many possibilities.
The choices we make
Become our only true
Compasses.

I could be here.
Or, I could be somewhere not here
With some other people
In some other country
In some other climate
On some other trajectory.
Was this always meant to be?
Or this just how it is?
My mouth becomes
Increasingly more parched.

As I sit here
Getting my mani/pedi done,
In anticipation of
A glass of ice-cold,
Clean, bottled water,
I acknowledge that —
Anxiety chose me.
No matter where I am
Or what I'm doing
Or who I'm with.
The unease that spreads
Like a wild forest fire,
Rages on.

LOSS
Charleston, South Carolina

Even the suspended elegance
Of the Spanish moss
From the ancient oak trees
In the dawning light,
Could not ameliorate
This year's grief.

THE LAST SUPPER
Brooklyn, New York
35th Birthday; Day I of IVF injections
Day 0, Covid-19 Pandemic (NYC closed the next day)

I apply
The blood-red
Lipstick.

I stick myself
In the stomach —
Twice.

I chew on
Birthday cake and
Uncertainty.

I swallow
The sweet vermouth and
Fear.

I wonder —
Is this our
Last supper?

WHAT WAS LOST & WHAT WAS GAINED
Brooklyn, New York
Day II of IVF
Day I, Self-Quarantine, Covid-19 Pandemic

I.

I got my first period
On Mother's Day.
I remember
The look on
My mother's face
But I don't remember
The innocence
Of not feeling pain.

My first gyno appointment
Was soon after.
My school absences
Piled up.
Each month became
A new physical reckoning
Testing my pain threshold.

My first time
In stirrups
I was so young;
It was nauseating.
The cold metal
Pushed inside my body
In that sterile exam room,
I was in a nightmare.
Now, I'm acclimated —
A reality I know all too well.

That first doc put me
On the pill
Without further investigation.
I hated those fucking chemicals.
The cramps
Hardly diminished

Instead, my personality did.
I felt numb--
A shadow of myself.
I still have
This image of the family
Dog sitting with me,
Licking my face
To comfort me.

II.

I sat
On the toilet,
Naked and screaming
As my body shook
Feeling my period's arrival.
No, the pill certainly
Was no remedy
For this dark disease.

Sometimes, when
I was younger
And afraid to be alone
With my uterus,
I would phone my Nana
To come over
With her heating pad
In hopes of providing me
Some relief.
Just being around
Her took some edge off.
During those years
I dipped into
Many different chemicals
At the bequest of doctors.
Migraines and moodiness
Was all I got in return.
I try to block out--
Those earlier
Bloody days.

III.

Once, while working
In Taipei,
I found myself in a
Non-English speaking
Health clinic.
I laid down in the
Familiar torture chair.
And rather abruptly,
My vagina appeared,
Magnified on a big screen.
As the instruments entered,
The doctor pointed out
All my anatomical
Lady parts.

A throng of nurses watched
As if spectators,
Voyeurs to my discomfort.
I felt like a science project.
She pointed out 2 cysts
But unsurprisingly,
Indicated no treatment
Or guidance.
I left feeling
Alone,
Defeated.
I went back to the hotel
Clenching my jaw,
Alternating Advil and Tylenol —
Maximum dose
As usual.

My college years
Must be buried
Deep, deep, deep.
I still only see
Blurs in my memory.
I refused more
Birth control pills,

Patches or otherwise.
I freed myself from
The prison
Of a hormonally controlled
Mind and body.
Though, peers
remind me
How often they
Found me
Writhing on the floor,
Enduring nature's
Monthly trauma.

IV.

I do recall
When it went
From very bad
To even worse.
The shock and awe pain
Came when I hit thirty.
I finally realized
My body was
Not always mine.
I projectile puked,
I passed out in alleys,
I dropped to my knees
Begging Gods
And Goddesses
To end my torment.

The first surgery,
Got the grapefruit-size
Cyst removed.
No white flag for my pain though.
Only a few months later,
Lesions and adhesions
Returned
With a spiteful vengeance.
I grit my teeth and
Tried to make-believe

I was healing.
No such luck.

A year later,
Deja-vu style,
I found myself
Under warm blankets,
Hooked up to the IV
On the surgery bed.
This second lap,
Four treacherous hours.
I'm no longer
A stranger to
Waking up shivering
And bloated
And bleeding
And groggy
And mad
And dizzy
From surgery.
It's never pretty.

Day by day
I got strong,
Again.
I welcomed
A thought—
Maybe this time
The battle
Is over?

Then, one night
I woke up
And couldn't move
My insides torqued
And twisted.
I had a kidney stone
Stuck inside of me.
Black lesions
On my ureters
Made it such a stubborn bitch.

It required two surgeries.

V.

Honestly,
Everything happens
For a reason.
Those surgeries,
Number four and five,
Triggered number six.
Because the battle inside
Wasn't finished.
My new surgeon,
Waged his own war
Against the turmoil.
He did his best,
He was a good soldier.
But another circle
Around the sun,
The internal terrorism persisted —
I had surgery
Lucky 7.
Doc put up a real fight.
But really,
There is still,
No winning.

The pain still forces me
To feel angst
Towards my elegant
Skeleton.
It's not a great look
For a dancer.
I try to smile.
Mostly,
I endure.

VI.

I didn't know that
One day

I might really
Want a baby
In my life,
In my arms,
In my shattered womb.
The time came—
Angels encouraged me.
My heart listened.
My body didn't.
I found another warrior —
This new, brave doc
Probed and prodded me
For weeks.
Finally, he tells me
What I already knew
From that first Mother's Day:
There is no natural
Way for me to
Conceive babies.
Endometriosis has
taken
taken
taken
taken
taken
taken
taken
taken
taken
taken
And taken more.

VII.

I write this
With profound gratitude.
I lost more
Than predicted
Or fathomed.
The floodgates of

Grief
Are always open.
But —
I found hope.
In IVF needles.
In the functional body parts.
In some doctors.
In many nurses.
In love.
In devotion.
In new chapters.
In empathy.
In the mountains
And the valleys.
The truth is
We can turn
Any devastation
On its head.
By using
Our hearts.

HAUNTED

Brooklyn, New York
Day III of IVF injections
Day II, Self Quarantine, Covid-19 Pandemic

These nights
When my bones
Feel hopelessly weary
And the moonlight signals
A time for peace,
My mind remains
Relentlessly
Alert.
As if sleep
Means falling
Uncontrollably
Headfirst into
A danger zone.
But then I
Readily realize
Reality is
The unpredictable
Dream that worries me
Awake.

WINDOWS
Brooklyn, New York
Day VIII of IVF
Day VII, Stay at Home Policy, Covid-19 Pandemic

Imagine life
Without windows...
Be grateful —
We can always
Let the light in.
A bounty
Of beauty
Beyond the pane.

RUNNING TO RUN FROM
Charleston, South Carolina
Day XXX Quarantine, Covid-19 Pandemic

The slap thwack smack whack
Of concrete striking my soles
Renders my nimble body, stiff.
Historically speaking,
I am no runner.
But once in a blue moon,
Unforeseen circumstances and
Force majeures,
Force my hand —
I pound the pavement
Hard and obsessively.

About a decade ago now,
On a posh London row,
I was involved with a man,
Who was too self-involved.
One dreary, misty morning,
I laced up my never before
Used kicks — my props
For a magic trick.
I dragged myself outside.
Hitting the ground in circles —
My great escape where I
Disappear into thin air.

Into the late winter,
Even when the thermostat,
And my bones,
Nearly shattered from the freeze,
I persisted.
My muscles,
Distraught and rigid,
Screamed for me to stop;
Begged for repose.
Even some polite Brit
Reprimanded me from his
Polished vehicle:

"A wee too cold for that, eh love?"

Without the strength
To break up and break free,
All of the sudden and
Over months and months,
Running became my religion.
I felt sick with guilt,
If I missed a single mile.
No amount of contrition or prayer
Could pardon the sin of a rest day.
The newly worn down trainers (sneakers!),
Laurels of something mimicking
Self-worth and stamina.
Hail the rotting rubber, full of grace,
Bless'ed were thee.
Eight months later,
We finally all called it quits,
Me and the narcissist,
Me and the church of jogging.

Today, I sit here,
Sweat dripping onto the keyboard.
I've taken to the streets, again.
Second time in my very active life.
Historically speaking,
I am no runner.
Only this unprecedented global pandemic with
A stay at home lockdown order,
(And that psychopath)
Could make me
Make a run for it.

MUFFINS & SELF-INTERROGATION
Charleston, South Carolina
Month V, Covid-19 Pandemic

Good morning darling,
Are you feeling
Threatened by
The languid ooze
Of loneliness?
Deeply demoralized
By the deafening
Regret of what
A superstar you
Could have been?
Do you feel
Terrorized by
The ennui
Of a morning walk;
Or the simplicity
Of your words?

Tell me,
Do you feel
Belittled by
Technology's chokehold?
Dehumanized by
The oversaturated
Onslaught of
Social media?
Strangled by
The impending
Decay of intimacy?
Disturbed by
The rot of connection
Between people
IRL?

Hey girl,
Do you feel
Abandoned by
Your country?

Are you exasperated by
The pervasive politics
Of your body,
Her body?
Or maybe you are,
Alarmed by
Your hostility
Towards taking
Your husband's name?
Have you been
Molested
Repeatedly by
The grimy hands
Of patriarchy's
Dirt?
Honey,
#me too.

Dear pisces,
Do you feel
Poisoned by
The process of
Aging?
Overwhelmed by
The new aches in
Your skeleton
And, the fresh wrinkles in
Your neck?
Are you ashamed
By the sudden
Disappearance of
Your sexual identity?
Do you still
Thirst after
Something you
Can't quite name?

about the author

Kate March is an American poet, performer, choreographer and painter. An internationally acclaimed artist, her multidisciplinary creative expressions have been praised as visionary, provocative, feminist, and emotionally courageous. She draws inspiration from raw emotion, travel experiences, intuition, the body, and the natural world. After living in London for 2 years, Hong Kong for 6 years and traveling the world extensively throughout that time, Kate now resides back home in America with her loving husband, Paul, and small, but mighty rescue dog, Bula. In June 2021, she begins her most adventurous chapter yet with the birth of their first child.

Discover more about Kate and her journey by checking out her website: www.katemarch.com and following her on Instagram @iam_katemarch. For more visual stories related to this book, please visit: www.thirstofpisces.com.

about atmosphere press

Atmosphere Press is an independent, full-service publisher for excellent books in all genres and for all audiences. Learn more about what we do at atmospherepress.com.

We encourage you to check out some of Atmosphere's latest releases, which are available at Amazon.com and via order from your local bookstore:

River Run!, poetry by Caitlin Jackson
Poems for the Asylum, poetry by Daniel J. Lutz
Licorice, poetry by Liz Bruno
Etching the Ghost, poetry by Cathleen Cohen
Spindrift, poetry by Laurence W. Thomas
A Glorious Poetic Rage, poetry by Elmo Shade
Numbered Like the Psalms, poetry by Catherine Phillips
Verses of Drought, poetry by Gregory Broadbent
Canine in the Promised Land, poetry by Philip J. Kowalski
PushBack, poetry by Richard L. Rose
Modern Constellations, poetry by Kendall Nichols
Whirl Away Girl, poetry by Tricia Johnson
Blue, poetry by Gülru Gözaçan
The Heroin Addict's Mother, poetry by Miriam Greenspan
Golden Threads, poetry by Uranbileg Batjargal
Quitting Time, poetry by Patrick Cabello Hansel
all the things my mother never told me, poetry by Daniella Deutsch
This Woman is Haunted, poetry by Betsy Littrell
Aching to Be Human, poetry by Stormy Abel
Impression, poetry by Charnjit Gill
Wind Bells, poetry by Jessica Dimalibot
How It Shone, poetry by Katherine Barham

CPSIA information can be obtained
at www.ICGtesting.com
Printed in the USA
LVHW092107050821
694330LV00020B/139